MW00896762

DIANA LEVINE KNITS
HATS & WINTERWEAR

ISBN: 9798857947807
Written, photographed, designed and edited by: Diana Levine

Contact:
dianalevineknits.com
instagram.com/dianalevineknits

TABLE OF CONTENTS

SUPPLIES & NOTES

All trademarks are used for clarification purposes only, and **do not imply** endorsement by the trademark owners.

KNITTING MACHINES
The patterns in this book refer to 22, 46 and 48 needle circular knitting machines. **22 needle circular knitting machines** that are compatible with these patterns include the Addi® Express Professional knitting machine and the Sentro™ or Jamit™ 22 needle knitting machines. **46 needle circular knitting machines** that are compatible with these patterns include the Addi® Express Kingsize knitting machine. **48 needle circular knitting machines** that are compatible with these patterns include the 48 needle Sentro™ or 48 needle Jamit™ knitting machine.

SIZING
The sizing of the patterns in this book will vary depending on your yarn, machine, and tension. You may need to knit more or fewer rows for your particular yarn and tension.

YARN
The hats, mittens, cowls and scarves in this book were created using Loops & Threads® Impeccable™ yarn, and Heartland™ yarn from Lion Brand Yarn®.

Yardage will vary depending on your tension. The projects shown here used 1 skein (approximately 251 to 285 yards each) or less in each color per project (except for the single-color 300 row scarf, and the single-color medium and large Horizontal Stitch hats, which required 2 skeins); however, you may need more or less yarn depending on your own tension. Please refer to the manual of your particular knitting machine for suggestions on which weight yarn will work best for your machine.

CRAFT SUPPLIES
You'll also need: crochet hook, darning needle, tape measure, stitch markers, scissors and pom pom makers. You can also use faux fur pom poms for the hats. Knitting tags are also included in many of these projects, which can be ordered online.

WELCOME

Dear reader,

Thank you so much for ordering "Hats & Winterwear", patterns for 22, 46 and 48 needle circular knitting machines!

With the projects in this book, you'll be able to create matching winter sets including hats, mittens, scarves and cowls. You can see some examples of matching winter sets knit with the patterns in this book on **Page 48**.

"Adjustable Width Knitting Machine Hats" is a pattern where you can choose the width of your hats based on how many rows you knit, in order to create a larger knitting machine hat. The "Horizontal Stitch Hats" are a warmer spin on the same concept, with a fold-up brim. The "Striped Hats" are a creative way to design various striped designs and styles.

The hats shown in this book are designed as an alternative to traditional knitting machine hats, where the stitches are running vertically. With a traditional knitting machine hat, you can adjust the height easily, but can only adjust the width significantly by switching to a knitting machine with more or fewer needles. With the hats in this book, you can easily adjust the width by knitting more or fewer rows (but can only adjust the height by changing to a machine with more or fewer needles).

Below, you can see the difference between a traditional knitting machine hat on the left, and the hats shown in this book (with the stitches running horizontally) on the right.

Traditional knitting machine hat

"Adjustable Width" knitting machine hats

The hats shown in this book require more time to seam and assemble than a traditional knitting machine hat. They require both grafting and seaming usng the Mattress Stitch. Both styles are fun to make and functional—try both methods and see which you prefer. You can find many tutorials for how to knit a traditional knitting machine hat online, on YouTube

and social media. (For reference, the traditional knitting machine hat shown in the previous photo is a 140 row fold-up brim hat, knit with a 46 needle circular knitting machine).

Please keep in mind that the patterns in this book are **not intended for use** by small children or infants. And the projects shown here may not be suitable for sale.

If you enjoy this book, you may also enjoy my other circular knitting machine pattern books, some of which are shown below. You can find these books on Amazon by searching for their titles, or visit dianalevineknits.com for links to all of my available pattern books.

If you make any projects using this book, please share them with me! You can find me **@dianalevineknits** on social media, on Instagram, YouTube, Facebook, Etsy, and Pinterest. I hope this book inspires many warm and cozy winter sets!

With gratitude,
Diana

Circular Knitting Machine Patterns Volume 1

Circular Knitting Machine Patterns Volume 2

Circular Knitting Machine Patterns Volume 3

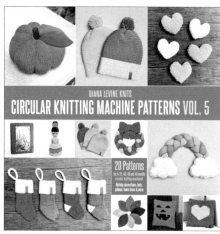

Circular Knitting Machine Patterns Volume 5

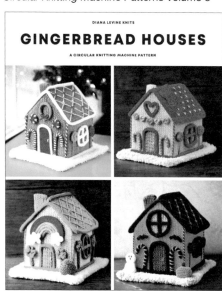

Gingerbread Houses: A Circular Knitting Machine Pattern

For a full list of available knitting machine pattern books and workbooks, please visit dianalevineknits.com.

Knitting Machine Techniques

In this section, you'll find instructions for three common techniques used with circular knitting machine pieces: seaming the ends, seaming using the Mattress Stitch, and the Duplicate Stitch.

Seaming The Ends Closed

Cast on and off with 5 rows of scrap yarn. Before you begin seaming, gently stretch out the stitches. Place the piece so that the yarn tails are on the left side of the work.

Identify the first line of stitches in the main color. You'll know which line of stitches to work through because it will be the very top line of main color stitches, directly above 1 line of scrap yarn stitches.

Begin seaming with the stitch all the way to the right side of the piece. This stitch will be perpendicular to the stitches to it's left side.

Then, thread through the loop **directly to it's left, on the top side.**

Pull that loop through.

Then, thread through the loop **directly to it's left, on the bottom side.**

Pull that loop through.

Continue back and forth between these steps. Soon, you'll see a seam beginning to form between the two sides.

Continue until the end of the row. Then, pull the yarn tail through the last loop.

Remove the scrap yarn. That side is now seamed. Repeat the same process again on the other side of the piece, making sure the stitches are running straight from one end to the other before seaming.

The Mattress Stitch

The Mattress Stitch is used to join together two pieces of knitting. It creates a seamless join between two pieces or edges.

When seaming two pieces with stitches running in the same direction, bring the two pieces together.

Identify the two lines of V-shaped stitches that you'll be joining. Make sure that the lines are running in the same direction.

Thread one of the yarn tails onto a darning needle. When working the stitches, thread through the interior bars to the **interior sides** of the two lines you selected above.

Thread through an interior bar on one side, and pull the yarn through.

Then, thread through an interior bar on the other piece, and pull the yarn through.

Continue back and forth between these steps, pulling tightly as you work. Soon, you'll see a seamless join forming.

Continue until the end. When you reach the end, secure the yarn with a knot.

Then, weave any remaining yarn tails into the center layer.

If you'd like to speed up the process, you can work the Mattress Stitch **two interior bars at a time.**

Stitches facing each other
If you'd like to seam pieces where the stitches are facing each other, alternate between one V-shaped stitch on one side, followed by one V-shaped stitch on the other side, pulling the yarn gently as you work.

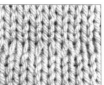

Stitches in different directions
For pieces where the stitches are facing opposite directions, alternate between one V-shaped stitch on one side, with one or two interior bars on the other side. Switch back and forth between one or two interior bars as you work, to keep the seam even.

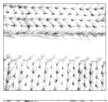

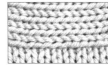

The Duplicate Stitch

To work the **Duplicate Stitch**, cut a long length of yarn in the color you'd like to use for your design. Secure the yarn with a knot on the back or inside of your project, and thread the yarn onto a darning needle.

To begin the stitch, thread the yarn out to the front of the work, exiting **below the stitch** you'd like to cover.

Pull the yarn through.

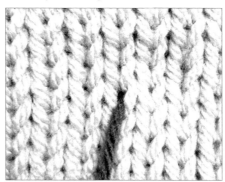

Next, thread the yarn from **right to left** through the V-shaped stitch **above** the stitch you want to cover. When you're working, **do not pull the yarn tightly.**

While you work, don't pull tightly, so that there is plenty of yarn to cover the stitch.

Pull the yarn through gently.

Next, thread the needle back through the hole **below** the stitch you're covering. When you exit the yarn, exit **below the next stitch** you'd like to cover.

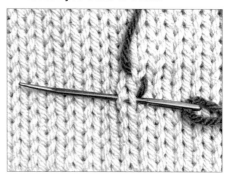

Pull the yarn through gently.

Your first Duplicate Stitch is now complete. Follow the same process again to work the next stitch.

Continue in the same process until you've finished your desired number of stitches. When you're done, thread to the back and secure with a knot.

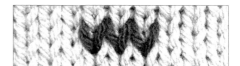

Tips: When working the Duplicate Stitch, it's **easier** to work **left to right**, or **right to left**, and then **bottom to top.** When you're reading a chart, look for ways to complete the chart by working horizontally, or bottom to top (avoiding working from top to bottom). Keep an eye on tension—make sure not to pull the yarn too tightly to ensure it covers the full stitch. And if you're working with double layered knitting, **only work through the top later**, not both layers of knitting.

ADJUSTABLE WIDTH HATS

These hats use a 22 needle circular knitting machine for the brim, and a 46 or 48 needle circular knitting machine for the top section. You can make the hat narrower by knitting fewer rows, or wider by knitting more rows.

SUPPLIES

- ☐ 22 needle circular knitting machine
- ☐ 46 or 48 needle circular knitting machine
- ☐ Weight 4/Medium yarn
- ☐ Darning needle
- ☐ 3.5" pom pom maker
- ☐ Knitting tag (optional)

QUICK RECIPE

SIZE SMALL:
- 22 needle circular knitting machine
- Cast on and off with scrap yarn
- **Knit 85 rows**

- 46 or 48 needle knitting machine
- Cast on and off with scrap yarn
- **Knit 85 rows**

SIZE MEDIUM:
- 22 needle circular knitting machine
- Cast on and off with scrap yarn
- **Knit 90 rows**

- 46 or 48 needle knitting machine
- Cast on and off with scrap yarn
- **Knit 90 rows**

SIZE LARGE:
- 22 needle circular knitting machine
- Cast on and off with scrap yarn
- **Knit 95 rows**

- 46 or 48 needle knitting machine
- Cast on and off with scrap yarn
- **Knit 95 rows**

NOTES:
These hats are designed as an alternative method to create circular knitting machine hats, which are traditionally knit with the stitches running vertically. Because the stitches are running horizontally in this hat, you can **adjust the width easily** by knitting more or fewer rows. If you'd like an **Extra Large Size** hat, simply knit more rows (you could try 100 or more rows, for example).

The height of the hat will remain the same, unless you switch to a different machine. The hats shown here were knit with the 46 needle Addi® Express Kingsize and

Professional knitting machines. If you use a 48 needle knitting machine for the top section, the hat will be slightly taller. Similarly, if you use a 40 needle circular knitting machine for the top section, the hat will be shorter.

Sizing for these hats will vary from person to person and yarn to yarn, as does head size. Please use the row counts as a guide, but knit up a few samples and try them on to see if you'd like to adjust the row counts based on your sizing and tension.

It's important for this project to have a clean seam with the grafting and the Mattress Stitch. When **grafting**, make sure to keep an **even tension**, and match the tension of the stitches above and below.

When working the **Mattress Stitch** to seam the two pieces together, make sure to bring together two lines of stitches running in the same direction, and continue along the same line of stitches from beginning to end. It's important to follow along the same line from beginning to end, so that the seam doesn't look twisted.

When knitting the two pieces, try to use a **similar tension** when knitting each piece, so that the tension is similar to each other.

If you adjust the row counts, make sure to use the **same number of rows for both pieces**. For example, if you knit 100 rows for the brim, knit 100 rows for the top section of the hat as well.

Important note: When you work the Mattress Stitch seam between the pieces, make sure **not to pull the yarn too tightly**. As you work the Mattress Stitch, keep **stretching out the hat with your hands while you seam**, to make sure that the seam is stretchy. Double check the seam is stretchy enough before securing the yarn with a knot to finalize the hat.

SIZING:
The sizing of these hats will vary depending on your yarn and tension.

Size Small: Approx. 8" wide x 9" tall
Size Medium: Approx. 8.5" wide x 9" tall
Size Large: Approx. 9" wide x 9" tall

Size Small
STEP 1: KNITTING THE BRIM
Cast on to a **22 needle circular knitting machine** with scrap yarn. **Knit 5 rows in the scrap yarn**. Switch to the brim color yarn, leaving a very long yarn tail (at least 45" long) in the main color yarn. **Knit 85 rows in the brim color yarn** (grey, in the example shown here). Switch back to the scrap yarn, again leaving a long yarn tail in the brim color. **Knit 5 rows in the scrap yarn**. Cut the scrap yarn and continue knitting until the work falls off the needles. Pull the knitting out of the machine and gently stretch out the stitches.

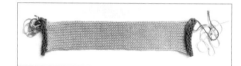

STEP 2: GRAFTING THE BRIM STITCHES
The next step is to **graft the stitches** from both ends of the knitting together. Grafting will create a **seamless join**.

Bring the two open ends of the work together, with the **yarn tails on the right side**. Thread the long yarn tail from the top side onto a darning needle.

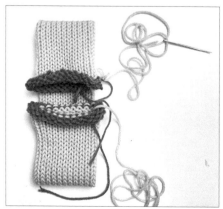

Begin grafting with two stitches on the bottom side of the work. You'll be working through two loops on the **top layer of the bottom section.**

Thread the darning needle **down** through a stitch on the bottom section, directly below where the yarn is emerging. Then, thread **up** through the stitch directly to it's left.

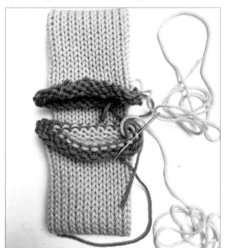

Then, gently pull the yarn through. When grafting the stitches, **do not pull the yarn tightly.** You are creating a new stitch with the grafting, and you want this stitch to be similar in size to the stitches directly above and below it. This will help give it a seamless look. To achieve this, don't pull the yarn tightly, and leave enough yarn in the stitch that it matches the size of the stitches in the main piece of knitting.

Then, go back to the top section, and work through the stitch directly above the previous stitch.

Thread **down** through the stitch, and then thread **up** through the stitch directly to it's left.

Pull the yarn through very gently.

On the next round, thread down **through the stitch you previously exited from** on that row, and then **up through the stitch directly to it's left.**

Pull the yarn through.

Then, go back to the top and **thread down through the stitch you previously exited from** on that row, and then **up through the stitch directly to it's left.**

Pull the yarn through.

Continue back and forth between these steps, pulling very gently while you work. Soon, you'll see a line of stitches beginning to form between the two ends.

Continue grafting until you reach the side.

You've now grafted one half of the work.

Turn the piece inside out. The open side of the work will now be facing up.

Continue in the same grafting process to seam this side from right to left.

When you reach the other side, make sure to capture every last remaining main color stitch. This is important so the piece doesn't unravel and there isn't a hole in the seam.

After you've captured all the last remaining main color stitches, secure the yarn tails with one quick knot.

Then, carefully remove the scrap yarn by unwinding around and around the work.

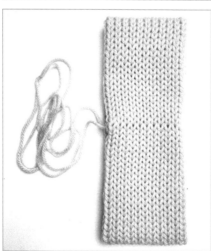

After the scrap yarn is removed, finalize the knot with the two yarn tails with a double knot. Turn the work over, with the grafted seam on the back. **Use the grafted side as the back of the hat.**

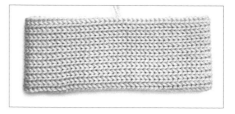

Note: If you prefer not to graft stitches, you can still make this hat; however, the seam may not look as seamless. If you prefer not to graft, simply use a crochet hook to seam the ends closed (like when making a scarf). Then, seam the two ends together in your preferred seaming method, and place the seamed side on the back of the hat.

STEP 3: KNITTING THE TOP SECTION
Cast on to a **46 or 48 needle circular knitting machine** using scrap yarn. **Knit 5 rows in the scrap yarn.** Switch to the main color yarn (purple, in the example shown here), leaving a very, very long yarn tail in the main color (at least 70') to use later when grafting. **Knit 85 rows in the main color yarn.** Switch back to the scrap yarn, leaving another long yarn tail. **Knit 5 rows in the scrap yarn.**

Cut the yarn and continue knitting until the work falls off the needles. Pull the knitting out of the machine and gently stretch out the stitches.

Note: As you work, try to **match the same tension** that you used when knitting the brim piece. You want the stitches to be the same size in the brim and top section, so try to use a yarn in the exact same size, and use a similar tension. **If you adjust the row counts, make sure to use the same row count for both pieces.**

STEP 4: GRAFTING THE TOP STITCHES

Next, follow the same directions as in **Step 2** to graft the ends together. The only difference is that this is a larger piece of knitting, so the process will take a little longer, and it will use more yarn, so you'll need a longer yarn tail.

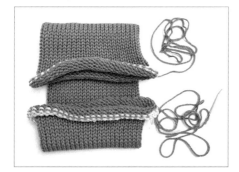

The grafting for the top section is now complete. Place both pieces with the back side (the grafted seam) **facing up**.

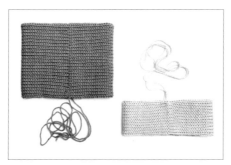

The top and bottom sections are now fully grafted and the hat is ready to assemble.

STEP 5: SEAMING THE BRIM AND TOP PIECES TOGETHER

Next, use the **Mattress Stitch** to seam the brim piece to the top piece.

Place both pieces with the **grafted seam facing up**. (You'll know which side has the grafted seam because it will have the yarn tails).

Weave 3 of the yarn tails into the center layer of the work. Thread the remaining yarn tail onto a darning needle. Choose either a yarn tail at the bottom of the top piece, or the yarn tail at the top of the bottom piece.

Place the top piece above the brim piece. **Line up the grafted seams together** in the same place. This will be the back of the hat.

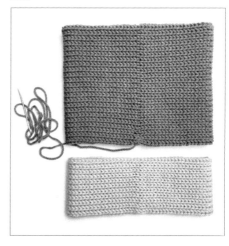

For this project, it's very important to create a clean seam with the Mattress Stitch. To achieve this, identify a line of V-shaped stitches **running in the same direction** on each side.

When you work the Mattress Stitch, work through the interior bars to the interior sides of these lines.

Using the yarn tail from the top piece, thread through two interior bars directly above the line you identified above.

Pull the yarn through.

Then, thread through two interior bars directly below the line you identified on the top piece earlier.

Pull the yarn through.

Continue back and forth between these steps. As you work, **don't pull the yarn too tightly.** Pull it through, but **give it a stretch every couple of inches** to make sure that the seam is stretchy enough to feel comfortable when worn. The yarn should be pulled firmly enough to seam the pieces together cleanly, but not so tight that the seam isn't stretchy enough to fit on someone's head.

Soon, you'll see a seamless join beginning to form between the two pieces.

Continue seaming until you reach the side, remembering to give the work a little stretch every couple of inches to make sure the seam is stretchy enough.

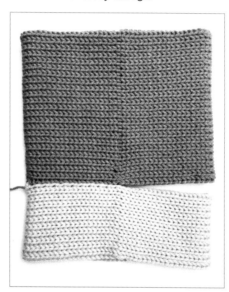

Then, flip the piece around, and continue seaming with the Mattress Stitch around the corner, and across the front of the hat.

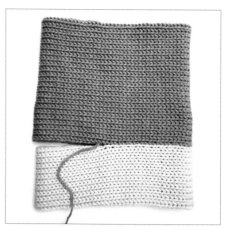

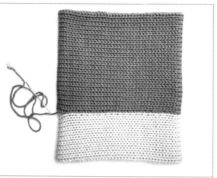

Next, turn the work back over so that the back of the hat is facing up, and continue seaming around the corner, and back to where you began the seam.

When you reach the end of the seam, make sure to capture every last remaining stitch to ensure there isn't a hole in the back of the hat.

Thread the yarn tail into the center of the hat, and secure the yarn with a knot on the inside of the hat. It's important to make this knot on the **inside**, rather than the outside, so it doesn't create a bump on the back of the hat.

After you've secured the yarn with a few good knots, weave the yarn tails into the center layer of the work.

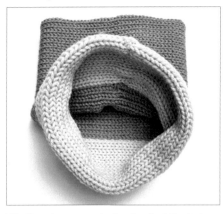

Flip the piece over to the front of the hat. The two pieces are now seamed together.

STEP 6: CINCHING THE TOP
Cut a long length of yarn in the same color as the top section of your hat. Thread the yarn onto a darning needle.

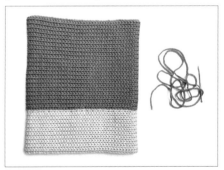

Use the length of yarn to create a **"drawstring"** around the top of the hat.

Along the top edge of the hat, thread **over and under** the interior bars between the lines of stitches.

Pull the yarn through.

For **visualization purposes only**, this is how the "drawstring" looks with a contrasting color. However, for your project, use the same color yarn as the top of the hat.

Continue all the way along the top.

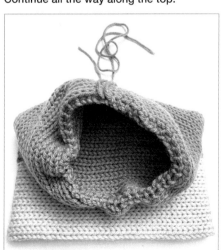

Cinch the top closed as tightly as you can with the yarn tails, and secure the yarn tails with a few good knots.

The top may still have a small hole remaining where you cinched the work.

Thread one of the yarn tails into the center layer of the knitting to hide the tail. Thread the remaining yarn tail onto a darning needle and use it to seam over any remaining hole at the cinched area.

Thread through one stitch on one side of the closure.

Pull the yarn through.

Then, thread through one stitch on the other side of the closure.

Pull the yarn through.

Continue back and forth along the closure until the top is fully seamed closed.

Secure the yarn with a few good knots on the inside of the hat and weave in the yarn tails into the center layer of the work.

The base of the hat is now complete.

If preferred, add a knitting tag.

STEP 7: ADDING A POM POM
If you'd like to add a pom pom as shown here, use a 3.5" pom pom maker.

Securely attach the pom pom to the top of the hat, and weave in any remaining yarn tails into the center layer of knitting. If preferred, add a knitting tag to the brim. Your Size Small "Adjustable Width Knitting Machine Hat" is now complete!

The **Size Medium** hat measures approximately 8.5" wide x 9" tall.

STEP 1: KNITTING THE PIECES

The Brim: Cast on to a **22 needle circular knitting machine** with scrap yarn. **Knit 5 rows in the scrap yarn**. Switch to the brim color yarn, leaving a very long yarn tail (at least 45" long) in the main color yarn.

Knit 90 rows in the brim color yarn (grey, in the example shown here). Switch back to the scrap yarn, again leaving a long yarn tail in the brim color. **Knit 5 rows in the scrap yarn.**

Cut the scrap yarn and continue knitting until the work falls off the needles. Pull the knitting out of the machine and gently stretch out the stitches.

Top section: Cast on to a **46 or 48 needle circular knitting machine** using scrap yarn. **Knit 5 rows in the scrap yarn.** Switch to the main color yarn (turquoise, in the example shown here), leaving a very, very long yarn tail in the main color (at least 70') to use later when grafting. **Knit 90 rows in the main color yarn.** Switch back to the scrap yarn, leaving another long yarn tail. **Knit 5 rows in the scrap yarn.**

Cut the yarn and continue knitting until the work falls off the needles. Pull the knitting out of the machine and gently stretch out the stitches.

Note: As you work, try to **match the same tension** that you used when knitting the brim piece.

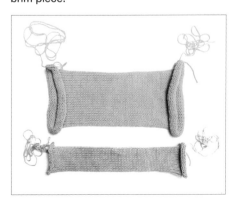

STEP 2: ASSEMBLING THE HAT

Follow all the same instructions as the **Size Small** hat shown previously to graft the stitches together, seam the two pieces together with the Mattress Stitch, cinch the top and seam over any remaining hole, and add a pom pom and/or kniting tag.

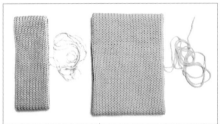

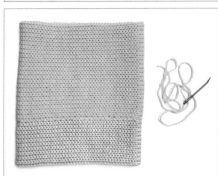

Size Large

The Size Large hat measures approximately 9" wide x 9" tall.

STEP 1: KNITTING THE PIECES
The Brim: Cast on to a **22 needle circular knitting machine** with scrap yarn. **Knit 5 rows in the scrap yarn.** Switch to the brim color yarn, leaving a very long yarn tail (at least 45" long) in the main color yarn. **Knit 95 rows in the brim color yarn** (grey, in the example shown here). Switch back to the scrap yarn, again leaving a long yarn tail in the brim color. **Knit 5 rows in the scrap yarn.**

Cut the scrap yarn and continue knitting until the work falls off the needles. Pull the knitting out of the machine and gently stretch out the stitches.

Top section: Cast on to a **46 or 48 needle circular knitting machine** using scrap yarn. **Knit 5 rows in the scrap yarn.** Switch to the main color yarn (yellow, in the example shown here), leaving a very, very long yarn tail in the main color (at least 70') to use

later when grafting. **Knit 95 rows in the main color yarn.** Switch back to the scrap yarn, leaving another long yarn tail. **Knit 5 rows in the scrap yarn.**

Cut the yarn and continue knitting until the work falls off the needles. Pull the knitting out of the machine and gently stretch out the stitches.

Note: As you work, try to **match the same tension** that you used when knitting the brim piece.

STEP 2: ASSEMBLING THE HAT
Follow all the same instructions as the **Size Small** hat shown previously to graft the stitches together, seam the two pieces together with the Mattress Stitch, cinch the top and seam over any remaining hole, and add a pom pom and/or knitting tag.

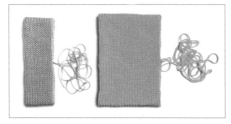

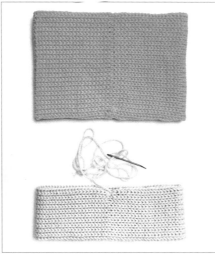

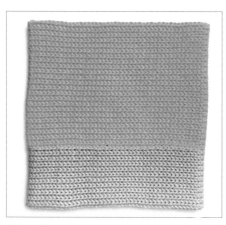

A Note About the Yarn
For this project, the yarn weight will affect the width of the hat. A yarn that has more stretch to it will require fewer rows than a yarn with less stretch. For example, when knitting an 85 row hat with one brand of yarn, the hat may measure 8" wide. Whereas with a different brand of yarn, using the exact same pattern and row count, it could measure 8.5" or 9" wide. Therefore, it's important with this project to knit up a sample hat in your particular yarn, and try it on, in order to get a feeling for how many rows you'd like to use for your hats, with your particular yarn and tension.

STRIPED HATS

These striped hats are adapted from the "Adjustable Width Knitting Machine Hats" pattern on Page 6. They are a fun way to use up leftover yarn scraps, or to create interesting patterns and designs.

SUPPLIES

- ☐ 46 or 48 needle circular knitting machine
- ☐ 22 needle circular knitting machine
- ☐ Weight 4/Medium yarn
- ☐ Darning needle
- ☐ Pom Pom maker (3.5"/9cm)
- ☐ Knitting tag (optional)

QUICK RECIPE

Follow the instructions on **Page 6** for the full explanation of how to make these hats. Then, use these details for how to knit the **top section.**

2X2 STRIPES:
- 46 or 48 needle knitting machine
- Cast on and off with scrap yarn
- *Knit 2 rows the main color, Knit 2 rows in the contrasting color* and repeat from * to * until your preferred number of rows, ending with 1 row of the contrasting color. Leave a very long yarn tail in the contrasting color.

SCRAP YARN HATS:
- 46 or 48 needle knitting machine
- Cast on and off with scrap yarn
- Knit 2 rows in each color until you reach your preferred number of rows, ending with 1 row in your last color. Leave a very long yarn yarn in the last color yarn.

RAINBOW HAT:
- 46 or 48 needle knitting machine
- Cast on and off with scrap yarn
- *Knit 2 rows of red, knit 2 rows of orange, knit 2 rows of yellow, knit 2 rows of green, knit 2 rows of blue, knit 2 rows of purple* 6 times. Then, knit 2 rows of red, knit 2 rows of orange, knit 2 rows of yellow, knit 2 rows of green, knit 2 rows of blue, and knit 1 row in purple. (83 rows in total) Leave a long yarn tail in the purple to use when grafting.

NOTES:
The yarn used in these striped hats is *Heartland™* yarn from Lion Brand Yarn®. Try mixing different colors when you create the pom poms, to match the hat!

2X2 STRIPES

For the style hat shown above, choose the number of stitches for your hat, based on the preferred width as shown in the "Adjustable Width Knitting Machine Hats" pattern on **Page 6.** If you'd like the stripes to match up correctly on the back, make sure to choose a row count that ends with 1 row of the contrasting color. For example: 83, 87, or 91 rows will all end on 1 row of the contrasting color.

For hat shown in these instructions, the **main color** yarn is black, and the **contrasting color** yarn is orange.

Top section:
Cast on to a **46 or 48 needle circular knitting machine** using scrap yarn. **Knit 5 rows in the scrap yarn.** Switch to the main color yarn (black, in the example shown here). *Knit 2 rows in the main color. Knit 2 rows in the contrasting color.* Repeat from * to * until you reach your preferred number of rows for your hat, **ending with 1 row in the contrasting color.** (In the hat shown here, there are 83 rows in total, with the 83rd row being orange). Switch back to the scrap yarn, **leaving a very, very long yarn tail (at least 70") in the contrasting color yarn. Knit 5 rows the scrap yarn.** Cut the yarn and continue knitting until the work falls off the needles.

When you work 2x2 stripes, you don't need to cut the yarn each time you switch colors. Instead, you can place the previous color yarn into the center of the knitting machine while you work the alternate color. Make sure to twist the yarn around the previous yarn color before switching to

---

the next yarn color. As you continue knitting, you'll see a twisted line of stitches running vertically down the knitting inside the machine, as shown here:

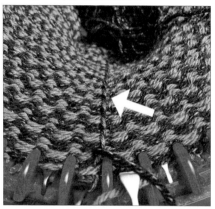

Brim:
Cast on to a **22 needle circular knitting machine** using scrap yarn. **Knit 5 rows in the scrap yarn.** Switch to the main color yarn (black, in the example shown here), leaving a very, very long yarn tail (at least 45") in the main color. **Knit the same number of total rows as you used in the top section** (in this example, 83 rows). Switch back to the scrap yarn. **Knit 5 rows in the scrap yarn.** Cut the yarn and continue knitting until the work falls off.

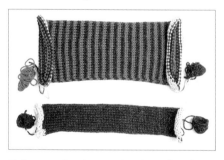

Before you begin seaming, turn the piece with the stripes inside out and secure any remaining yarn tails with knots and trim the tails. (Do not knot the yarn tails between the scrap yarn and the cast on and cast off yarn tails).

Then, follow all the same instructions as seen in the "Adjustable Width Knitting Machine Hats" pattern on **Page 6** to graft the ends of each piece together.

When grafting the 2x2 stripes, make sure to **use the long yarn tail from the cast off side.** The grafted seam will create an additional row—so you want to make sure to use the same color yarn as your last row of stitches.

In this example, the piece ended on 1 row of orange. So, the long orange yarn tail will be used to graft the pieces together, which will create the look of the 2nd orange row after it's seamed together.

Above, you'll see that grafting with the contrasting color (orange, in this example) creates the 2nd row in the last stripe.

Continue following all the same instructions as in the "Adjustable Width Knitting Machine Hats" pattern on Page 6 to finish grafting the ends of both pieces, and then seam the pieces together, cinch the top, and add a pom pom and knitting tag.

SCRAP YARN HATS

These hats are a fun way to use up scrap yarn you've gathered. As you work on other projects, save the ends of skeins of yarn, and then use them to make a hat once you've saved up enough scrap yarn.

For the style hat shown above, choose the number of stitches for your hat based on the preferred width as shown in the "Adjustable Width Knitting Machine Hats" pattern on **Page 6.**

Top section:
Cast on to a **46 or 48 needle circular knitting machine** using scrap yarn. **Knit 5 rows in the scrap yarn.** Switch to the first color yarn. **Knit 2 rows in each color until you** reach your preferred number of rows for your hat, ending with 1 row on your last stripe. Switch back to the scrap yarn, leaving a very, very long yarn tail (at least 70") in the last yarn color. **Knit 5 rows the scrap yarn.** Cut the yarn and continue knitting until the work falls oft the needles.

Brim:
Cast on to a **22 needle circular knitting machine** using scrap yarn. **Knit 5 rows in the scrap yarn.** Switch to the main color yarn (black, in the example shown here), leaving a very, very long yarn tail in the main color (at least 45"). **Knit the same number of total rows as you used in the top section.** Switch back to the scrap yarn. **Knit 5 rows in the scrap yarn.** Cut the yarn and continue knitting until the work falls off the needles.

When you work with so many different colors, there will be many yarn tails in the center of the work. Before you begin seaming, turn the top section inside out and secure all the yarn tails tightly with knots and trim the tails. (Do not knot the yarn tails between the scrap yarn and the cast on and cast off yarn tails).

Then, turn the work right side out and follow all the same instructions as in the "Adjustable Width Knitting Machine Hats" pattern on Page 6 to graft the ends of both pieces, seam the pieces together, cinch the top, and add a pom pom and knitting tag.

Note: When working with so many yarn tails, one side of the piece may end up a little bumpier than the other. Use this side as the top of the hat, since it will be cinched together at the end.

RAINBOW HATS

Top section:
Cast on to a **46 or 48 needle circular knitting machine** using scrap yarn. **Knit 5 rows in the scrap yarn.** Switch to the red yarn. ***Knit 2 rows in Red. Knit 2 rows in Orange. Knit 2 rows in Yellow. Knit 2 rows In Green. Knit 2 rows in Blue. Knit 2 rows in Purple*** and repeat from * to * 5 more times **(6 total)**. Then, **knit 2 rows in Red. Knit 2 rows in Orange. Knit 2 rows in Yellow. Knit 2 rows in Green. Knit 2 rows in Blue.** *Knit 1 row in Purple*. (83 rows in total). Switch back to the scrap yarn, leaving a very, very long yarn tail (at least 70") in the purple yarn. **Knit 5 rows in the scrap yarn.** Cut the yarn and continue knitting until the work falls off the needles.

If you'd like a larger hat, you can add an additional repeat of the first rainbow pattern, as long as you end on 1 row of purple for your last repeat.

Brim:
Cast on to a **22 needle circular knitting machine** using scrap yarn. **Knit 5 rows in the scrap yarn.** Switch to the main color yarn (black, in the example shown here), leaving a very, very long yarn tail (at least 45") in the main color. **Knit the same number of total rows as you used in the top section** (in this example, 83 rows). Switch back to the scrap yarn. **Knit 5 rows in the scrap yarn.** Cut the yarn and continue knitting until the work falls off the needles.

Then, follow all the same instructions as in the "Adjustable Width Knitting Machine Hats" pattern on **Page 6** to graft the ends, seam the pieces together, cinch the top, and add a pom pom and knitting tag.

Horizontal Stitch Hats

These hats are made using the same technique as the "Adjustable Width Hats" on Page 6; however, the bottom section is created with a 46 or 48 needle circular knitting machine, in order to create a fold-up brim.

Supplies

- ☐ 46 or 48 needle circular knitting machine
- ☐ Weight 4/Medium yarn
- ☐ Darning needle
- ☐ 3.5" pom pom maker
- ☐ Knitting tag (optional)

Quick Recipe

SIZE SMALL:
- 46 or 48 needle circular knitting machine
- Cast on and off with scrap yarn
- **Knit 85 rows**
(Knit 2)

SIZE MEDIUM:
- 46 or 48 needle circular knitting machine
- Cast on and off with scrap yarn
- **Knit 90 rows**
(Knit 2)

SIZE LARGE:
- 46 or 48 needle circular knitting machine
- Cast on and off with scrap yarn
- **Knit 95 rows**
(Knit 2)

NOTES:
These hats are made with the **same instructions** as the "Adjustable Width Knitting Machine Hats" on Page 6. The **only difference** is that you'll knit **both pieces with the 46 or 48 needle circular knitting machine** (rather than knitting the bottom piece with a 22 needle circular knitting machine). Then, you'll **fold up the brim** from the bottom section.

Like the "Adjustable Width Knitting Machine Hats", these hats are designed to be an alternative method to creating a hat on a circular knitting machine. Traditionally, circular knitting machine hats are created with the stitches running vertically, which means that the width is somewhat fixed, while you can change the height with the row count. Alternatively, in these hats, the height is somewhat fixed, but you can **choose the width** easily by knitting more or

fewer rows. The height of the hat will remain the same, unless you switch to a different machine. The hats shown here were knit with the 46 needle Addi® Express Kingsize knitting machine. If you use a 48 needle circular knitting machine, the hat will be slightly taller. Similarly, if you use a 40 needle circular knitting machine for the pieces, the hat will be even shorter.

Sizing for these hats will vary from person to person and yarn to yarn, as does head size. Please use the row counts as a guide, but **knit up a few samples** and try them on to see if you'd like to adjust the row counts based on your sizing and tension.

It's important for this project to have **clean seams** with the grafting and the Mattress Stitch. When grafting, make sure to keep an **even tension**, and match the tension of the stitches above and below.

When working the Mattress Stitch to seam the two pieces together, make sure to bring together two lines of stitches **running in the same direction**, and continue along the **same line of stitches** from beginning to end. It's important to follow along the same line from beginning to end, so that that seam doesn't look twisted.

When knitting the two pieces, try to use a **similar tension** when knitting each piece, so that the tension is similar to each other.

If you adjust the row count for this project to create smaller or larger hats than shown here, make sure to use the same row count for both pieces of knitting.

Important note: When you work the Mattress Stitch seam between the pieces, make sure **not to pull the yarn too tightly**. As you work the Mattress Stitch, keep **stretching out the hat with your hands while you seam**, to make sure that the seam is stretchy.

SIZING:
The sizing of these hats will vary depending on your yarn and tension. The approximate sizing of the hats shown here:

Size Small: Approx. 8.5" wide x 9" tall
Size Medium: Approx. 9.5" wide x 9" tall
Size Large: Approx. 10.5" wide x 9" tall

STEP 1: KNITTING THE PIECES
Cast on to a **46 or 48 needle circular knitting machine** using scrap yarn. **Knit 5 rows in the scrap yarn.** Switch to the main color yarn, leaving a very, very long yarn tail (at least 70") in the main color yarn.

Small: Knit **85 rows** in the main color.
Medium: Knit **90 rows** in the main color.
Large: Knit **95 rows** in the main color.

Then, switch back to the scrap yarn, again leaving a very long yarn tail in the main color yarn. **Knit 5 rows in the scrap yarn.**

Then, cut the scrap yarn and continue knitting until the work falls off the needles. Pull the work out of the machine and gently stretch out the stitches.

Repeat this process again to make a **second piece in the exact same row count.** You can either use the same color, or a different color for the second piece. If you use the same color, the hat will be single-color. If you use different colors, the brim will be a contrasting color.

Note: The project shown here is the Size Small (85 rows). If you'd like your hat to be narrower, knit fewer rows. If you'd like your hat to be wider, simply knit more rows. For reference, this hat was knit with a 46 needle circular knitting machine.

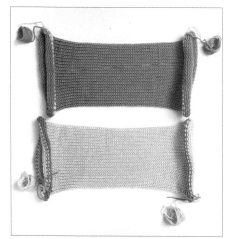

The next step is to graft the ends of the pieces together. If you've already made the "Adjustable Width Knitting Machine Hat" on **Page 6**, you can follow all the same instructions, and simply fold up the brim after the hat is complete.

STEP 2: GRAFTING THE ENDS

The next step is to graft the ends of the knit tube together. Place your piece vertically, and fold the bottom and top up together so that the open ends are facing each other, with the yarn tails to the right side.

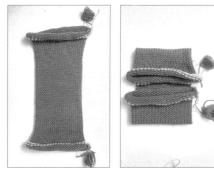

Thread the long yarn tail from the bottom side onto a darning needle.

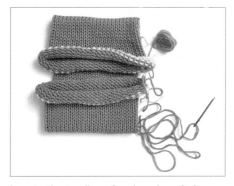

Locate the top line of main color stitches on the edge of the top piece. Begin working through the stitches directly above where the yarn tail is emerging from on the bottom piece.

Thread **down through the first stitch**, and then **up through the stitch to it's left.**

Pull the yarn through **very gently**. While you're grafting, leave enough yarn that it replicates the tension of the stitches above and below the grafted seam.

Then, go back down to the bottom piece. Thread **down through the stitch immediately below**, and then **up through the stitch to it's left.**

Pull the yarn through very gently.

Then, go back to the the top piece. Repeat the stitch again; however, this time, thread down through the same stitch that you **previously exited from** when you last worked the top row.

Pull the yarn through very gently.

Then, go back down to the the bottom piece. Repeat the stitch again; however, this time, thread down through the same stitch that you **previously exited from** when you last worked the bottom row.

And pull the yarn through very gently.

Continue back and forth between these steps, remembering to pull the yarn **gently** so that the tension of the grafted seam matches the stitches above and below. Soon, you'll see a seam forming between the two pieces.

Continue grafting until you reach the other side of the work. Then, turn the piece inside out, so that the remaining open seam is facing up.

Continue in the same process as earlier to continue seaming around the open edge of the tube, until you reach where you began the grafted seam. Secure the yarn tails with a couple of good knots.

Then, remove the scrap yarn by unwinding around and around the work.

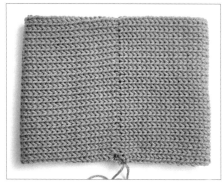

The first piece is now grafted and ready to assemble into the hat. Next, repeat the exact same process again to graft the ends of the other piece together.

Both pieces are now grafted and ready to assemble into the hat. Place the pieces with the **grafted seam facing up**, as shown in the image below. Line up the pieces so that the grafted seams are lined up on top of each other. This will be the **"back" side** of the hat.

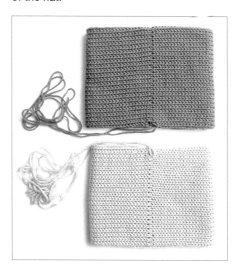

STEP 3: SEAMING THE PIECES TOGETHER

The next step is to seam the two pieces together. Begin by threading three of the long yarn tails into the center layers of the knitting to hide the tails. Thread the remaining yarn tail onto a darning needle. If you are using two different colors (such as in this example) you can use the lighter color yarn for seaming, so it's less likely to show through the knitting.

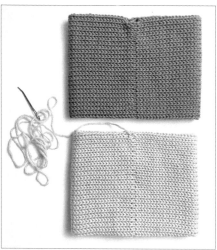

Next, use the **Mattress Stitch** to seam the pieces together. First, make sure the stitches aren't twisted. Then, identify one line of V-shaped stitches on either piece that are running in the same direction that you'd like to bring together using the Mattress Stitch.

As you work the Mattress Stitch, thread through the interior bars to the interior sides of these lines.

It's **very important** for this project to create a **clean seam**. To achieve a clean seam, make sure to follow the exact same line of stitches from beginning to end, without twisting the work.

It's also **very important** to **stretch the Mattress Stitch seam every couple of inches** to make sure that the seam is stretchy enough to be worn. If you seam too tightly, the hat will not be stretchy enough to wear as a hat. So, make sure to give the seam a good stretch regularly.

Thread through two interior bars on the edge of the opposite side from where the yarn tail is emerging.

Pull the yarn through gently.

Then, thread through two interior bars on the edge of the other piece.

Pull the yarn through gently.

Continue back and forth between these steps. Soon, you'll see a seam beginning to form between the two pieces.

After a couple of inches, stop seaming and **give the seam a good stretch**. You want the seam to be tight enough to keep the pieces together cleanly—but not so tight that it makes the hat too tight to wear. Pause seaming every couple of inches, give the seam a stretch, and then continue.

Continue seaming until you reach the side.

Then, turn the work around and continue seaming across the "front" of the hat.

Then, turn the work back to the "back" of the hat, and continue seaming until you reach where you began the seam. Continue to stretch the seam as you work.

When you reach where you began the seam, make sure to capture every last remaining stitch, so that there isn't a hole at the back of the hat.

After your seam is finished, thread the yarn into the center of the hat, and secure the yarn with a knot on the **inside** of the hat.

It's important to knot the yarn on the inside, so that there isn't a knot on the outside of the back of the hat.

The pieces are now seamed together.

STEP 4: CINCHING THE TOP

Turn the work over to the "front" of the hat. Cut a long length of yarn in the color you used for the top section and thread the yarn onto a darning needle.

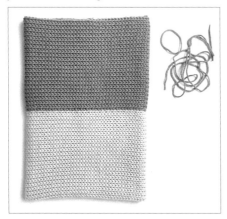

To cinch the top, create a "drawstring" around the top open edge of the hat using the length of yarn.

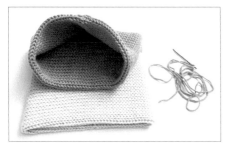

To create the "drawstring", thread over and under all the interior bars at the edge.

For visualization purposes only, here is how the "drawstring" looks using a contrasting color. (However, for your project, use the same color as the hat).

Add the drawstring using the same color as your hat, as shown here:

Use the two yarn tails to cinch the top closed tightly, and secure with a few good knots. Make sure to roll the work in as you cinch the top.

If there is any hole remaining, you can use the yarn tails to sew over the hole at the top. Then, thread the yarn tails into the center layer of the knitting to hide the tails.

STEP 5: FINAL TOUCHES

Lay out the hat as shown here, and then flip the bottom piece up halfway to create the brim.

If preferred, add a knitting tag to the cuff.

To add a pom pom, use a 3.5cm pom pom maker to create a pom pom, and attach it to the top-center of the hat.

Weave in any remaining yarn tails into the center layer of the knitting. Your Horizontal Stitch Hat is complete!

Single-Color Hats

If you'd like to create a "Horizontal Stitch Hat" all in the same color, such as the hat shown in the image on the next page, follow all the same instructions as shown on Pages **20-25**, except use the same color for both pieces.

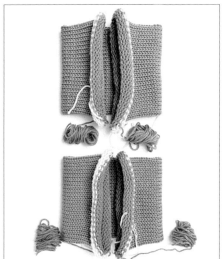

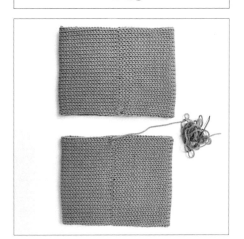

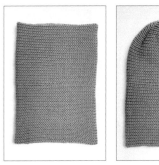

Sizing Note

Keep in mind that the hats may stretch out a bit over time. So you may want to err on the side of slightly smaller rather than larger with the row counts. And make sure to continually stretch the Mattress Stitch seam while you work so that it remains stretchy enough to wear.

Back of the hats

As shown earlier, place the grafted seam as the back of the hat. For reference, here are some photos of the front and back of the hats.

Front of the hat

Back of the hat

Sizing

Here are "Horizontal Stitch Hats" made using the Small, Medium, and Large sizing. Keep in mind that these were created using a Weight 4 yarn. Your hats may be smaller or larger, depending on your particular yarn and tension.

SIZE SMALL (85 rows):
Approximately 8.5" wide x 9.5" tall

SIZE MEDIUM (90 rows):
Approximately 9.5" wide x 9.5" tall

SIZE LARGE (95 rows):
Approximately 10.5" wide x 9.5" tall

HANDMADE BY
DIANA LEVINE

Family Sized Mittens

Knit up a matching set of mittens with this customizable pattern! Because these mittens are created with double-layered knitting, they are very warm and cozy for the winter.

Supplies

- ☐ 22 needle circular knitting machine
- ☐ 46 or 48 needle circular knitting machine
- ☐ Weight 4/Medium yarn
- ☐ Crochet hook
- ☐ Darning needle
- ☐ Stitch markers
- ☐ Knitting tags (optional)

Quick Recipe

ADULT SIZE LARGE
Main piece (Knit 2):
- 46 or 48 needle knitting machine
- Cast on with scrap yarn
- Cast off with main color yarn
- **Knit 20 rows in the cuff color**
- **Knit 45 rows in the main color**

Thumb piece (Knit 2):
- 22 needle circular knitting machine
- Cast on with scrap yarn
- Cast off with main color yarn
- **Knit 18 rows in the main color**

ADULT SIZE SMALL/MEDIUM
Main piece (Knit 2):
- 46 or 48 needle knitting machine
- Cast on with scrap yarn
- Cast off with main color yarn
- **Knit 20 rows in the cuff color**
- **Knit 40 rows in the main color**

Thumb piece (Knit 2):
- 22 needle circular knitting machine
- Cast on with scrap yarn
- Cast off with main color yarn
- **Knit 15 rows in the main color**

CHILDREN'S SIZE MEDIUM/LARGE
Main piece (Knit 2):
- 46 or 48 needle knitting machine
- Cast on with scrap yarn
- Cast off with main color yarn
- **Knit 20 rows in the cuff color**
- **Knit 35 rows in the main color**

Thumb piece (Knit 2):
- 22 needle circular knitting machine
- Cast on with scrap yarn
- Cast off with main color yarn
- **Knit 12 rows in the main color**

CHILDREN'S SIZE SMALL
Main piece (knit 2):
- 46 or 48 needle knitting machine
- Cast on with scrap yarn
- Cast off with main color yarn
- **Knit 20 rows in the cuff color**
- **Knit 30 rows in the main color**

Thumb piece (knit 2):
- 22 needle circular knitting machine
- Cast on with scrap yarn
- Cast off with main color yarn
- **Knit 10 rows in the main color**

SIZING NOTES:
The **Children's Size Small** is designed to fit approximately **ages 5 to 6 years old**. The **Children's Size Medium/Large** is designed to fit approximately **ages 7 to 9 years old**. For 10+ years, try using the **Adult Size Small/Medium** pattern.

This pattern is easily customizable in terms of sizing. Mitten sizing varies widely among people, so these row counts are a suggestion, but you may want to add or reduce rows depending on your yarn, tension, and hand size. If you are knitting a matching set while you are adapting the patterns, make sure to keep the **20-row cuff row count** the same—instead, add or remove rows from the **main color section** of the mitten, in order to keep the cuff sizes the same.

If you'd like to adjust the size of the thumb, simply knit more or less rows in the thumb piece. To adjust the width of the mittens, you can try knitting with looser or tighter tension, try different yarns, or use a different machine. The 48 needle Sentro™ knitting machine will create a slightly wider mitten than the 46 needle Addi® Express Kingsize knitting machine. For reference, the mittens shown here were knit with the 46 needle Addi® Express Kingsize knitting machine. I suggest knitting and assembling one mitten first to assess sizing, before knitting the second mitten.

If you'd like a **longer cuff**, add more rows to the cuff section. You could try 25 or 30 rows in the cuff color yarn (instead of 20). If you're knitting a matching set, make sure to use the **same cuff row count** for each pair.

Measurements:
Adult Size (Large): Approximately 10.5" tall, hand: 3.5" wide, thumb: 3.5" long.
Adult Size (Small/Medium): Approximately 9.5" tall, hand: 3.5" wide, thumb: 2.5" long.
Children's Size (Medium/Large): Approximately 8.5" tall, hand: 3.5" wide, thumb: 2.25" long.
Children's Size (Small): Approximately 7" tall, hand: 3.5" wide, thumb: 2" long.

Adult Size Large

The **Adult Size (Large)** mittens measure approximately 10.5" tall, 3.5" wide in the hand section, and 3.5" long thumb. Size will vary depending on yarn and tension.

STEP 1: KNITTING THE HAND PIECE
Cast on to a **46 or 48 needle circular knitting machine** using scrap yarn. **Knit 5 rows in the scrap yarn.** Switch to the cuff color yarn (grey, in the example shown here), leaving a long yarn tail to use when seaming later. **Knit 20 rows in the cuff color.** Switch to the main color yarn (blue, in the example shown here). **Knit 45 rows in the main color yarn.** Cut a long yarn tail and thread the tail onto a darning needle. Pick up all the stitches off the machine. (Do not use scrap yarn for the cast off).

Turn the work inside out and secure the yarn color change tails with a few good knots and trim the tails. Do not tie a knot between the scrap yarn and the first row of the cuff.

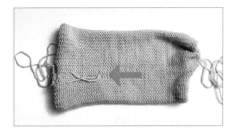

STEP 2: ASSEMBLING THE HAND PIECE

Use the yarn tail on the cast off end to cinch the work closed at the top off the mitten. Secure the cinch with a couple of good knots.

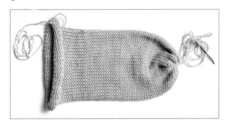

Next, use a crochet hook to seam the open end of the work closed (see Page 4 for details). Remove the scrap yarn.

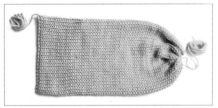

You'll now have a piece with one flat end (at the cuff) and one cinched end (at the top of the mitten). Fold the work in half.

If you find it helpful, you can add stitch markers in advance where you'll be creating the opening for the thumb (adding a stitch marker where you'll begin the opening and where you'll end the opening). You may adjust the location of these when you reach that area, so the locations don't need to be exact.

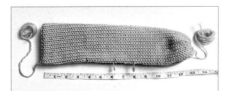

The first stitch marker shown here is placed **2" after the cuff**, and the second stitch marker is placed **1.5" after the first stitch marker.**

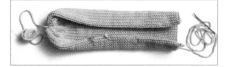

The next step is to seam the sides of the piece together. Thread the yarn tail from the cuff side onto a darning needle. Use the Mattress Stitch (see Page 4 for details) to begin seaming the sides together, working through two interior bars on one side, followed by two interior bars on the other side, until you reach 2" from the beginning of the cuff.

Before you begin, locate a line of V-shaped stitches **running in the same direction** on either side that you'll be bringing together with the Mattress Stitch.

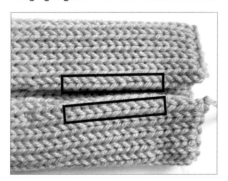

When you work the Mattress Stitch, thread through the bars to the interior sides of these lines.

To begin, thread through two interior bars on the opposite side from where your yarn tail is emerging and pull the yarn through.

Then, thread through two interior bars on the other side of the work and pull the yarn through tightly.

Continue back and forth between these steps, pulling the yarn firmly while you work. Soon, you'll see a seamless join forming between the two sides.

Continue seaming until you reach your first stitch marker.

At this point, if you are knitting the mittens for yourself, you can try the mitten on for size and see where you'd like the thumb hole to begin. If need be, you can adjust the location of the thumb hole to suit your preference by seaming longer or shorter than the 2" shown here.

When you're satisfied with the location of the thumb hole, remove the stitch marker and **secure the yarn with a knot** on an interior bar. Choose an interior bar that will end up being located on the **inside** of the thumb, and not the outside.

Next, thread the yarn tail through the stitches on one side of the work, and exit the darning needle approximately **1.5" from where you began the thumb hole.**

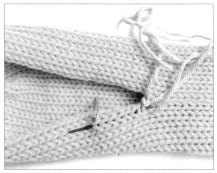

When you reach the area of the second stitch marker, remove the stitch marker.

Stretch the area of the thumb hole to make sure there's enough room for the thumb piece. Then, secure the yarn with a knot on an interior stitch (so that the knot will not show from the outside later after you add the thumb piece). It's **important** to make sure you stretch out this area before creating the second knot, so that it doesn't feel too tight when the mitten is worn.

Then, continue using the Mattress Stitch to seam the rest of the mitten, seaming all the way to the top of the mitten.

As you get closer to the top of the mitten (the cinched side of the work), it may become a little more challenging to follow along the same line of stitches if the work starts to roll. Keep rolling the work out as you seam, to make sure you're seaming along the same line of V-shaped stitches from beginning to end.

Make sure to capture all the last remaining stitches all the way to the cinched end of the mitten, to ensure there isn't a hole at the end of the mitten.

When you reach the end, secure the two yarn tails together with a few good knots, and weave the yarn tails into the center of the work.

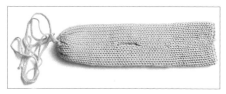

Then, weave the yarn tails into the center layer of the knitting and trim the tails.

The hand section of the mitten is now complete.

STEP 3: KNITTING THE THUMB

Cast on to a **22 needle circular knitting machine** using scrap yarn. **Knit 5 rows in the scrap yarn.** Switch to the main color yarn (blue, in the example shown here), leaving a long tail to use when seaming later. **Knit 18 rows in the main color yarn.** Then, cut a long yarn tail and thread it onto a darning needle. Pick up all the stitches off the machine. Pull the work out of the machine and gently stretch out the stitches.

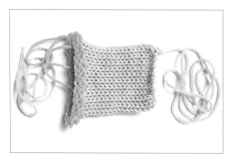

Cinch the top of the work closed and secure with a the yarn with a knot.

Next, use a crochet hook to seam the open end of the work closed (see Page 4 for details). Remove the scrap yarn.

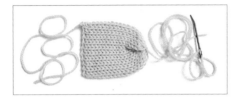

STEP 4: ASSEMBLING THE THUMB
Thread the yarn tail from the flat end onto a darning needle. Fold the piece in half. Use the Mattress Stitch to seam the sides together, beginning with the flat side, and working towards the cinched side of the piece.

Begin by identifying one line of V-shaped stiches running in the same direction on either side of the piece that you'll be bringing together with the Mattress Stitch.

Thread through two interior bars on one side, and pull the yarn through.

Then, thread through two interior bars on the other side, and pull the yarn through.

As when seaming the hand piece, make sure to continue seaming along the same

line of stitches all the way until the top of the cinched area.

As you near the end of the seam, make sure to capture all the remaining stitches to ensure there isn't a hole at the end of the thumb piece.

When you reach the cinched area, secure the yarn tails with a couple of good knots. If the piece is leaning towards the side a bit, that's okay—**seam the thumb with the leaning side towards the top of of the mitten.**

Weave in the yarn tails into the center layer of the work and trim the tails. Then, cut a new length of yarn in the mitten color yarn, secure it with a knot on the open edge of the thumb piece, and thread it onto a darning needle.

After you have a yarn tail ready to go at the open edge of the thumb piece, it's time to seam the thumb piece to the thumb hole on the hand piece.

STEP 5: ASSEMBLING THE MITTEN
You'll now have a finished hand piece and a finished thumb. The next step is to seam the thumb to the thumb hole.

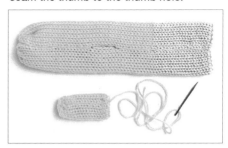

Before you begin, fold up the cuff on the hand piece.

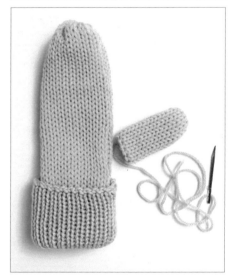

Place the area of the thumb with the seam facing the bottom of the mitten, so that it doesn't show from the top of the mitten when the mitten is worn.

Then, thread through one interior bar on the hand piece, at the edge of the thumb hole, and pull the yarn through.

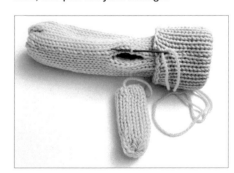

Then, thread through one V-shaped stitch on the edge of the thumb piece, and pull the yarn through.

On the next round, work through **two** interior bars on the hand piece, instead of one (as shown earlier).

Pull the yarn through.

Then, like earlier, thread through one V-shaped stitch on the edge of the thumb piece, and pull the yarn through.

Continue repeating these steps until you reach the side of the thumb piece. Alternating between one and two interior bars on the hand piece will help create a more even seam.

When you reach the side of the thumb hole, you'll need to switch the style of seaming to working through V-shaped stitches on both pieces. For both the top and bottom sides of the thumb piece, thread through one V-shaped stitch on the edge of the thumb piece, and pull the yarn through.

Then, thread through one V-shaped stitch on the edge of the thumb hole on the hand piece, and pull the yarn through.

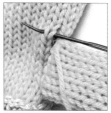 

After you round the corner, go back to the original seaming method, alternating between one or two interior bars on the hand piece, with one V-shaped stitch on the edge of the thumb piece.

When you round the corner to the final side of the thumb piece, go back to alternating between V-shaped stitches.

Then, turn the piece around and continue seaming the thumb piece until you reach where you began your seam. Make sure to capture every last remaining stitch, so there isn't a hole at the seam between the thumb hole and the thumb piece.

After the thumb is fully seamed into the mitten, thread the yarn tail into the inside of the mitten and **secure with a knot on the inside** of the mitten. Then, weave the yarn tail into the center layer of the work to hide the tail.

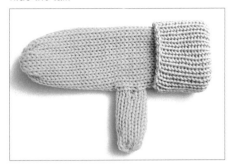

The mitten is now complete! Try on the mitten to see how it feels and if you'd like to make any adjustments before knitting the second mitten.

If preferred, add a knitting tag to the cuff of the mitten. Then, repeat the exact same process again, from **Step 1** to **Step 5**, to create the second mitten. There is no difference between the left and right mittens—simply turn the second mitten over before adding a knitting tag, so that the thumbs are on different sides.

The **Adult Size Small/Medium** mittens measure approximately 9.5" tall, 3.5" wide in the hand section, and a 2.5" long thumb.

STEP 1: KNITTING THE HAND PIECE
Cast on to a **46 or 48 needle circular knitting machine** using scrap yarn. **Knit 5 rows in the scrap yarn.** Switch to the cuff color yarn (grey, in the example shown

here), leaving a long yarn tail to use when seaming later. **Knit 20 rows in the cuff color.** Switch to the main color yarn (yellow, in the example shown here). **Knit 40 rows in the main color yarn.** Cut a long yarn tail and thread the tail onto a darning needle. Pick up all the stitches off the machine. (Do not use scrap yarn for the cast off).

STEP 2: ASSEMBLING THE HAND PIECE
Follow the directions in **Step 2** of the **Adult Size Medium/Large pattern** to seam and assemble the hand piece of the mitten.

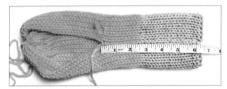
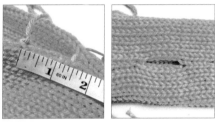

STEP 3: KNITTING THE THUMB
Cast on to a **22 needle circular knitting machine** using scrap yarn. **Knit 5 rows in the scrap yarn.** Switch to the main color yarn (yellow, in the example shown here), leaving a long tail to use when seaming later. **Knit 15 rows in the main color yarn.** Then, cut a long yarn tail and thread it onto a darning needle. Pick up all the stitches off the machine.

Cinch the top of the work closed and secure with a knot. Use a crochet hook to seam the open end of the tube. Remove the scrap yarn.

Next, follow the assembly instructions in **Step 3** of the **Adult Size Medium/Large pattern** to seam and assemble the thumb.

STEP 4: ASSEMBLING THE MITTEN
The hand and thumb piece are now complete and ready to assemble. Follow the instructions in **Step 4** of the **Adult Size Large pattern** to seam the thumb to the thumb hole on the hand piece.

Children's Size Medium/Large

The **Children's Size Medium/Large** mittens measure approximately 8.5" tall, 3.5" wide in the hand section, and a 2.25" long thumb. Size will vary depending on yarn and tension.

STEP 1: KNITTING THE HAND PIECE
Cast on to a **46 or 48 needle circular knitting machine** using scrap yarn. **Knit 5 rows in the scrap yarn.** Switch to the cuff color yarn (grey, in the example shown here), leaving a long yarn tail to use when seaming later. **Knit 20 rows in the cuff color.** Switch to the main color yarn (green, in the example shown here). **Knit 35 rows in the main color yarn.** Cut a long yarn tail and thread the tail onto a darning needle. Pick up all the stitches off the machine. (Do not use scrap yarn for the cast off).

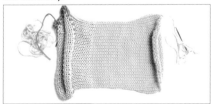

STEP 2: ASSEMBLING THE HAND PIECE
Follow the directions in **Step 2** of the **Adult Size Large pattern** to seam and assemble the hand piece.

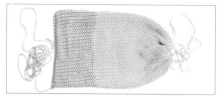

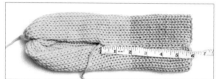

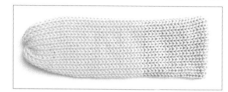

STEP 3: KNITTING THE THUMB
Cast on to a **22 needle circular knitting machine** using scrap yarn. **Knit 5 rows in the scrap yarn.** Switch to the main color yarn (green, in the example shown here), leaving a long tail to use when seaming later. **Knit 12 rows in the main color yarn.** Then, cut a long yarn tail and thread it onto a darning needle. Pick up all the stitches off the machine. Pull the work out of the machine and stretch out the stitches. Cinch the top of the work closed and secure with a the yarn with a knot.

Use a crochet hook to seam the open end of the tube. Remove the scrap yarn.

STEP 4: ASSEMBLING THE MITTEN
Next, follow the assembly instructions in **Steps 3 to 5** of the **Adult Size Large pattern** to seam and assemble the thumb and seam it to the hand piece.

Repeat the same process again, from **Step 1** to **Step 5**, to create the second mitten. Your Children's Size Medium/Large mittens are complete!

Children's Size Small
The **Children's Size Small** mittens measure approximately 7" tall, 3.5" wide in the hand section, with a 2" long thumb. Size will vary depending on yarn and tension.

STEP 1: KNITTING THE HAND PIECE
Cast on to a **46 or 48 needle circular knitting machine** using scrap yarn. **Knit 5 rows in the scrap yarn.** Switch to the cuff color yarn (grey, in the example shown here), leaving a long yarn tail to use when seaming later. **Knit 20 rows in the cuff color.** Switch to the main color yarn (purple, in the example shown here). **Knit 30 rows in the main color yarn.** Cut a long yarn tail and thread the tail onto a darning needle. Pick up all the stitches off the machine. (Do not use scrap yarn for the cast off).

STEP 2: ASSEMBLING THE HAND PIECE
Follow the directions in **Step 2** of the **Adult Size Large pattern** to seam and assemble the hand piece of the mitten.

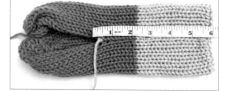

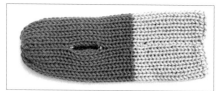

STEP 3: KNITTING THE THUMB
Cast on to a **22 needle circular knitting machine** using scrap yarn. **Knit 5 rows in the scrap yarn.** Switch to the main color yarn (purple, in the example shown here), leaving a long tail to use when seaming later. **Knit 10 rows in the main color yarn.** Then, cut a long yarn tail and thread it onto a darning needle. Pick up all the stitches off the machine. Cinch the top of the work closed and secure the cinch with a knot.

Use a crochet hook to seam the open end of the tube closed. Remove the scrap yarn.

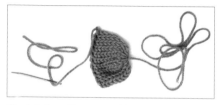

Next, follow the assembly instructions in **Step 3** of the **Adult Size Medium/Large pattern** to seam and assemble the thumb.

STEP 4: ASSEMBLING THE MITTEN
The hand piece and the thumb piece are now complete and ready to assemble. Follow the instructions in **Step 4** of the **Adult Size Large pattern** to seam the thumb to the thumb hole on the hand piece. Your mittens are now complete!

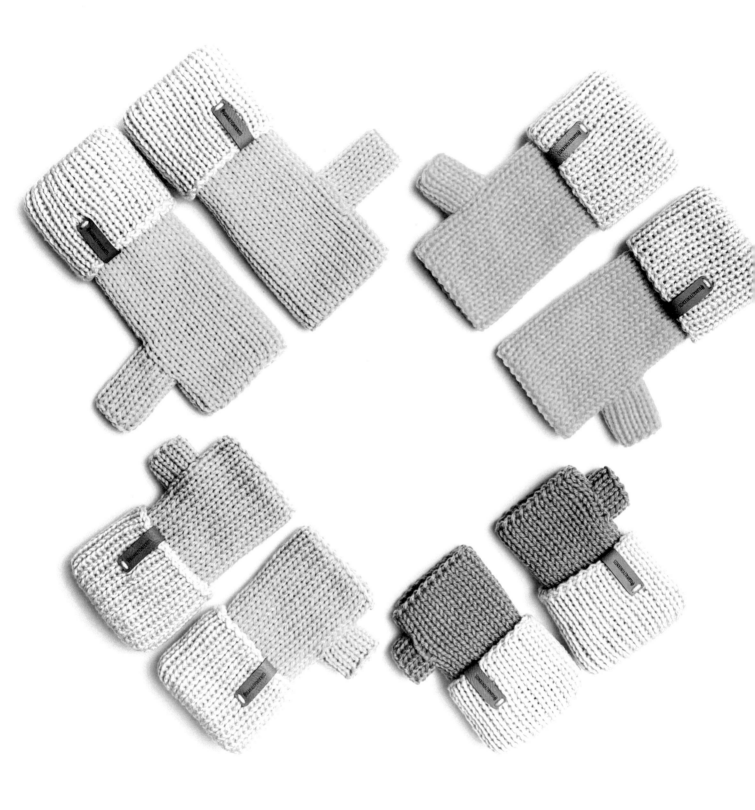

FINGERLESS MITTENS

These mittens are a bright and fun way to keep your hands warm! The sizes are easy to adapt to a variety of hand sizes by increasing or reducing the row counts.

SUPPLIES

- ☐ 46 or 48 needle circular knitting machine
- ☐ 22 needle circular knitting machine
- ☐ Weight 4/Medium yarn
- ☐ Crochet hook
- ☐ Stitch markers
- ☐ Darning needle
- ☐ Measuring tape
- ☐ Scissors
- ☐ Knitting tag (optional)

QUICK RECIPE

ADULT SIZE SMALL/MEDIUM:
Main piece (Knit 2):
- 46 or 48 needle circular knitting machine
- Cast on and off with scrap yarn
- **Knit 32 rows in the cuff color**
- **Knit 27 rows in the main color**

Thumb piece (Knit 2):
- 22 needle circular knitting machine
- Cast on and off with scrap yarn
- **Knit 11 rows in the main color**

ADULT SIZE LARGE:
Main piece (Knit 2):
- 46 or 48 needle circular knitting machine
- Cast on and off with scrap yarn
- **Knit 32 rows in the cuff color**
- **Knit 32 rows in the main color**

Thumb piece (Knit 2):
- 22 needle circular knitting machine
- Cast on and off with scrap yarn
- **Knit 14 rows in the main color**

CHILD SIZE SMALL:
Main piece (Knit 2):
- 46 or 48 needle circular knitting machine
- Cast on and off with scrap yarn
- **Knit 28 rows in the cuff color**
- **Knit 18 rows in the main color**

Thumb piece (Knit 2):
- 22 needle circular knitting machine
- Cast on and off with scrap yarn
- **Knit 6 rows in the main color**

CHILD SIZE MEDIUM:
Main piece (Knit 2):
- 46 or 48 needle circular knitting machine
- Cast on and off with scrap yarn
- **Knit 28 rows in the cuff color**
- **Knit 22 rows in the main color**

Thumb piece (Knit 2):
- 22 needle circular knitting machine
- Cast on and off with scrap yarn
- **Knit 8 rows in the main color**

SIZING NOTES:
The **Children's Size Small** is designed to fit approximately **ages 5 to 7 years old**. The **Children's Size Medium/Large** is designed to fit approximately **ages 7 to 10 years old**. For 10+ years, try using the **Adult Size Small/Medium** pattern.

This pattern is easily customizable in terms of sizing. Mitten sizing varies widely among people. These row counts are a suggestion, but you may want to add or reduce rows depending on your yarn, tension, and hand size.

If you'd like to adjust the length of the mittens, knit more or fewer rows. If you'd like to adjust the size of the thumb, you can also knit more or fewer rows.

To adjust the width of the mittens, you can try knitting with looser or tighter tension, try different yarns, or use a different machine. A 48 needle circular knitting machine will create a slightly wider mitten than a 46 needle knitting machine. For reference, the mittens shown here were knit with the 46 needle Addi® Express Kingsize knitting machine.

I suggest knitting and assembling one mitten first to assess sizing, before knitting the second mitten.

Measurements:
Adult Size Small/Medium: Approximately 8" long x 3.5" wide, thumb: 1.5" long
Adult Size Large: Approximately 9" long x 3.5" wide, thumb: 2.25" long
Children's Size Small: Approximately 6" long x 3.5" wide, thumb: 1" long
Children's Size Medium: Approximately 6.5" long x 3.5" wide, thumb: 1.25" long

Keep in mind that sizing will vary depending on the yarn you are using, as well as the tension and machine size. Please use these row counts as a suggestion; however, it's important to knit up some samples in your own yarn and tension to assess your preferred sizing.

The two mittens are made in the exact same way. However, place the thumb piece with the knots facing the back of each mitten, for a cleaner look.

Adult Size Small/Medium

These mittens measure approximately 8" long x 3.5" wide. The thumb measures approximately 1.5" long. Sizing will vary depending on yarn, tension and machine.

STEP 1: KNITTING THE MAIN PIECE
Cast on to a **46 or 48 needle circular knitting machine** using scrap yarn. **Knit 5 rows in the scrap yarn.** Switch to the cuff color yarn (light gray, in the example shown here), leaving a very long yarn tail in the cuff color yarn to use later when seaming. **Knit 32 rows in the cuff color yarn.** Switch to the main color yarn (yellow, in the example shown here). **Knit 27 rows in the main color yarn.** Switch back to the scrap yarn, again leaving a very long yarn tail in the main color yarn. **Knit 5 rows in the scrap yarn.**

Cut the yarn and continue knitting until the work falls off the needles. Pull the work out of the machine and gently stretch out the stitches.

Finalize the knot between the yarn color changes on the inside.

STEP 2: SEAMING THE ENDS
Use a crochet hook to seam the open ends of the work closed. Remove the scrap yarn.

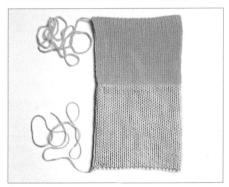

STEP 3: KNITTING THE THUMB PIECE
Cast on to a **22 needle circular knitting machine** using scrap yarn. **Knit 5 rows in the scrap yarn.** Switch to the main color yarn (yellow, in the example shown here), leaving a long yarn tail in the main color. **Knit 11 rows in the main color.** Switch back to the scrap yarn, again leaving another long yarn tail in the main color. **Knit 5 rows in the scrap yarn.**

Cut the yarn and continue knitting until the work falls off the needles.

STEP 4: SEAMING THE ENDS
Use a crochet hook to seam the open ends of the work closed. Remove the scrap yarn.

Both pieces of the mitten are now fully seamed and ready to assemble together.

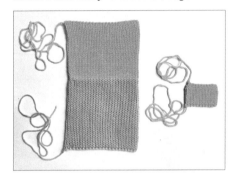

STEP 5: ASSEMBLING THE THUMB
Place the thumb piece with the yarn tails on the bottom side. Thread one of the long yarn tails onto a darning needle.

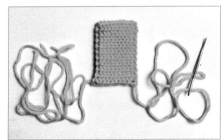

Fold the top and bottom sides together. If it helps, you can keep them in place temporarily with stitch markers.

Use the Mattress Stitch to seam the sides together. Thread through two interior bars on one side and pull the yarn through.

Then, thread through two interior bars on the other side of the work, and pull the yarn through.

Continue back and forth between these steps. Soon, you'll see a seamless join beginning to form between the sides.

Continue seaming with the Mattress Stitch until you reach the other end of the work. When you reach the end, secure the two yarn tails together with a few good knots.

Weave one yarn tail into the center layer of the work to hide the tail. Thread the remaining yarn tail onto a darning needle.

The thumb piece is now assembled and you can set the piece aside while you begin to assemble the main piece.

STEP 6: ASSEMBLING THE MAIN PIECE

Place the main piece with the yarn tails on the bottom side.

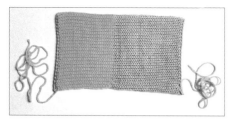

Fold the top and bottom sides together. If it helps, you can keep them in place temporarily with stitch markers.

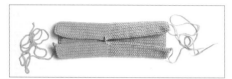

Thread the yarn tail from the cuff side onto a darning needle. Beginning with the cuff side, use the Mattress Stitch (as shown earlier in Step 4), to seam the piece together, working towards the main color.

It's important for this part of the project to create a clean seam. To achieve this, before you begin seaming, identify two lines of V-shaped stitches on either side that are **running in the same direction.** When you work the Mattress Stitch, thread through the interior bars to the interior sides of these lines.

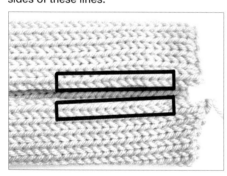

Thread through two interior bars on one side and pull the yarn through.

Then, thread through two interior bars on the other side, and pull the yarn through.

Continue back and forth between these steps, making sure to follow along the same line of V-shaped stitches from beginning to end. Soon, you'll see a seamless join beginning to form between the two sides.

Continue seaming until you reach the main color yarn.

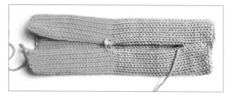

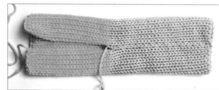

After you reach the main color, pause seaming. Next, use the thumb piece that was assembled earlier and identify where you'd like the thumb to be located.

If you're knitting the mitten for yourself, you can try on the mitten and use your own hand as a guide for where to place the thumb.

Place stitch markers at the top and bottom of where the thumb will be placed.

Then, continue seaming until you reach the first stitch marker.

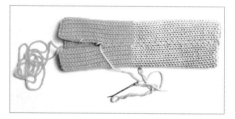

After you reach the first stitch marker, remove the stitch marker, and **secure the yarn with a knot.** Place the knot on a stitch that will end up being on the **inside of the mitten,** not on an outside stitch.

Then, thread the yarn through the stitches on one side of the work, until you reach the other stitch marker.

Like earlier, secure the yarn with a knot on a stitch that will end up being on the inside of the mitten. Before making this knot, **give the yarn a good stretch** to make sure there's plenty of yarn across, so that the thumb hole isn't too tight.

Then, go back to using the Mattress Stitch to finish seaming the rest of the mitten.

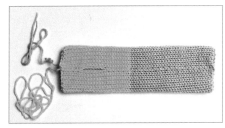

When you reach the end, secure the two yarn tails together with a couple of good knots.

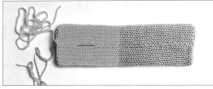

After the yarn tails are secured with knots, weave the yarn tails into the center layer of the work to hide the tails.

The location of the thumb hole will vary from person to person; however, for reference, the thumb hole for this mitten began **11 stitches from the cuff** and here are the measurements for each section:

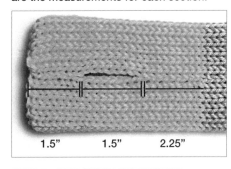

1.5"   1.5"   2.25"

STEP 7: ATTACHING THE THUMB

The next step is to seam the thumb onto the area of the thumb hole. If there is a little bump from where you knotted the yarn tails on the thumb piece, place that side of the thumb down, so it will be on the bottom of the mitten, rather than on the top side of the mitten.

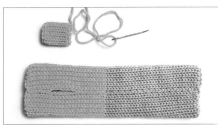

Place the thumb piece over the thumb hole, with the side with the knot facing what will be the bottom side of the mitten.

Beginning with the side that will end up being the bottom of the mitten, thread through one interior bar on the mitten piece and pull the yarn through.

Then, thread through one V-shaped stitch on the thumb and pull the yarn through.

On the next round, thread through two interior bars (instead of one) on the mitten piece and pull the yarn through.

Then, thread through one V-shaped stitch on the thumb piece and pull the yarn through.

Continue back and forth between these steps until you reach the corner of the thumb.

When you are seaming these sides of the thumbs, thread through one V-shaped stitch on the mitten piece and pull the yarn through.

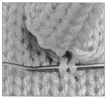 

Then, thread through one V-shaped stitch on the thumb piece and pull the yarn through.

Continue with this seaming method until you reach the other side of the thumb.

Then, go back to the seaming method shown on the previous page to alternate between one or two interior bars on the mitten piece, with one V-shaped stitch on the thumb piece, until you reach the next

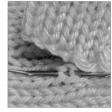 

When you turn the corner, go back to alternating between V-shaped stitches for the next few stitches.

When you turn the next corner, you'll be a few stitches away from completing the seam. Go back to the first seaming method, alternating between one or two interior bars on the mitten piece, with a V-shaped stitch on the thumb piece, until you complete the seam.

After the thumb is fully seamed, thread the yarn tail into the inside of the mitten, and secure the yarn with a few good knots on the inside of the mitten.

It's important to secure the extra few knots on the inside of the mitten, because it will look cleaner than knotting on the outside of the mitten.

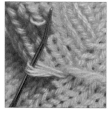 

Then, weave all remaining yarn tails into the center layer of the work.

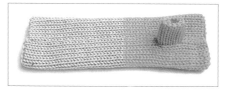

STEP 8: FOLDING UP THE CUFF
Place the mitten with the thumb to the side of the work, and then fold up the cuff.

If you'd like to add one, add a knitting tag to the cuff of the mitten. Next, repeat the entire process again to make the second mitten. When you place the thumb onto the second mitten, make sure to place the side with the knot facing the palm side of the mitten. Your Adult Size Small/Medium fingerless mittens are complete!

Adult Size Large

These mittens measure approximately 9" long x 3.5" wide. The thumb measures approximately 2.25" long. Sizing will vary depending on yarn, tension and machine.

STEP 1: KNITTING THE MAIN PIECE

Cast on to a **46 or 48 needle circular knitting machine** using scrap yarn. **Knit 5 rows in the scrap yarn**. Switch to the cuff color yarn (light gray, in the example shown here), leaving a very long yarn tail in the cuff color yarn to use later when seaming. **Knit 32 rows in the cuff color yarn**. Switch to the main color yarn (blue, in the example shown here). **Knit 32 rows in the main color yarn**. Switch back to the scrap yarn, again leaving a very long yarn tail in the main color yarn. **Knit 5 rows in the scrap yarn**.

Cut the yarn and continue knitting until the work falls off the needles. Pull the work out of the machine and gently stretch out the stitches.

Finalize the knot between the yarn color changes on the inside.

STEP 2: KNITTING THE THUMB PIECE

Cast on to a **22 needle circular knitting machine** using scrap yarn. **Knit 5 rows in the scrap yarn**. Switch to the main color yarn (blue, in the example shown here), leaving a long yarn tail in the main color. **Knit 14 rows in the main color**. Switch back to the scrap yarn, again leaving another long yarn tail in the main color. **Knit 5 rows in the scrap yarn**.

Cut the yarn and continue knitting until the work falls off the needles.

STEP 3: ASSEMBLING THE MITTENS

Follow **Steps 2 to 8** in the **Adult Size Small/Medium** mittens to seam the pieces and assemble the mittens.

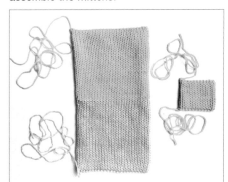

The location of the thumb hole will vary from person to person; however, for reference, the thumb hole for this mitten began **14 stitches from the cuff** and here are the measurements for each section:

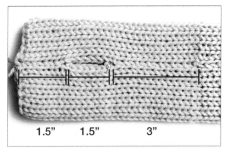

1.5"   1.5"   3"

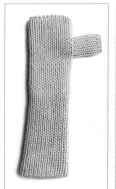

Then, repeat the same process again to make the second mitten in the same size.

If you'd like, add knitting tags to the cuffs. The Adult Size Large mittens are now complete!

Child Size Small

These mittens measure approximately 6" long x 3.5" wide. The thumb measures approximately 1" long. Sizing will vary depending on yarn, tension and machine.

STEP 1: KNITTING THE MAIN PIECE

Cast on to a **46 or 48 needle circular knitting machine** using scrap yarn. **Knit 5 rows in the scrap yarn**. Switch to the cuff color yarn (light gray, in the example shown here), leaving a very long yarn tail in the cuff color yarn to use later when seaming. **Knit 28 rows in the cuff color yarn**. Switch to the main color yarn (purple, in the example shown here). **Knit 18 rows in the main color yarn**. Switch back to the scrap yarn, again leaving a very long yarn tail in the main color yarn. **Knit 5 rows in the scrap yarn**. Cut the yarn and continue knitting until the work falls off the needles. Pull the work out of the machine and gently stretch out the stitches.

STEP 2: KNITTING THE THUMB PIECE
Cast on to a **22 needle circular knitting machine** using scrap yarn. **Knit 5 rows in the scrap yarn.** Switch to the main color yarn (purple, in the example shown here), leaving a long yarn tail in the main color. **Knit 6 rows in the main color.** Switch back to the scrap yarn, again leaving another long yarn tail in the main color. **Knit 5 rows in the scrap yarn.**

Cut the yarn and continue knitting until the work falls off the needles.

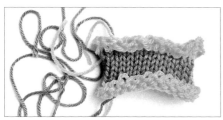

STEP 3: ASSEMBLING THE MITTENS
Follow **Steps 2 to 8** in the **Adult Size Small/Medium** mittens to seam the pieces and assemble the mittens.

The location of the thumb hole will vary from person to person; however, for reference, the thumb hole for this mitten began **6 stitches from the cuff** and here are the measurements for each section:

1"   1.25"   1.25"

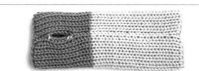

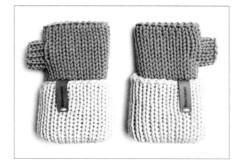

Children's Size Medium

These mittens measure approximately 6.5" long x 3.5" wide. The thumb measures approximately 1.25" long. Sizing will vary depending on yarn, tension and machine.

STEP 1: KNITTING THE MAIN PIECE
Cast on to a **46 or 48 needle circular knitting machine** using scrap yarn. **Knit 5 rows in the scrap yarn.** Switch to the cuff color yarn (light gray, in the example shown here), leaving a very long yarn tail in the cuff color yarn to use later when seaming. **Knit 28 rows in the cuff color yarn.** Switch to the main color yarn (green, in the example shown here). **Knit 22 rows in the main color yarn.** Switch back to the scrap yarn, again leaving a very long yarn tail in the main color yarn. **Knit 5 rows in the scrap yarn.**

Cut the yarn and continue knitting until the work falls off the needles. Pull the work out of the machine and gently stretch out the stitches.

STEP 2: KNITTING THE THUMB PIECE
Cast on to a **22 needle circular knitting machine** using scrap yarn. **Knit 5 rows in the scrap yarn.** Switch to the main color yarn (green, in the example shown here), leaving a long yarn tail in the main color. **Knit 8 rows in the main color.** Switch back to the scrap yarn, again leaving another long yarn tail in the main color. **Knit 5 rows in the scrap yarn.**

Cut the yarn and continue knitting until the work falls off the needles.

STEP 3: ASSEMBLING THE MITTENS
Follow **Steps 2 to 8** in the **Adult Size Small/Medium** mittens to seam the pieces and assemble the mittens.

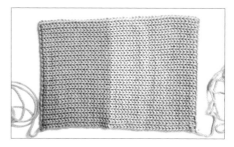

The location of the thumb hole will vary from person to person; however, for reference, the thumb hole for this mitten began **8 stitches from the cuff** and here are the measurements for each section:

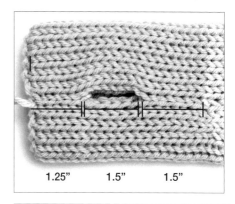

1.25"   1.5"   1.5"

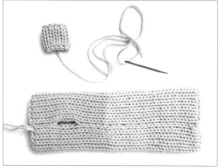

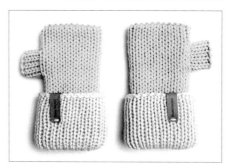

The Children's Size Large mittens are now complete!

Cowls and Scarves

Cowls and scarves are a very quick and easy project to make with a circular knitting machine. You can use a 40 needle, 46 needle, or 48 needle circular knitting machine to knit a cowl or scarf.

Supplies

- [ ] 40, 46, or 48 needle circular knitting machine
- [ ] Weight 4/Medium yarn
- [ ] Crochet hook
- [ ] Darning needle
- [ ] Knitting tags (optional)

Quick Recipes

SINGLE-COLOR COWL
- 40, 46, or 48 needle knitting machine
- Cast on and off with scrap yarn
- **Knit 200 rows in the main color**

TWO-TONE COWL
- 40, 46, or 48 needle knitting machine
- Cast on and off with scrap yarn
- **Knit 100 rows in the first color**
- **Knit 100 rows in the second color**

STRIPED COWL
- 40, 46, or 48 needle knitting machine
- Cast on and off with scrap yarn
- ***Knit 10 rows in the first color knit 10 rows in the second color* (and repeat from * to * until you reach 200 rows)**

SCARF
- 40, 46, or 48 needle knitting machine
- Cast on and off with scrap yarn
- **Knit 250-300 rows in the main color**

LONG STRIPED SCARF
- 40, 46, or 48 needle knitting machine
- Cast on and off with scrap yarn
- **Knit 20 rows in each color until you reach 300-400 rows.**

NOTES:
Scarves and cowls are a commonly knit project using circular knitting machines! The row counts listed above are just suggestions—you can easily customize these cowls and scarves by knitting more or fewer rows, in any variety of color combinations or different style stripes. For reference, all of the cowls and scarves shown here were knit with a 46 needle circular knitting machine (except for the Long Striped Scarf, which was knit with a 40 needle circular knitting machine).

TWO-TONE COWL:
Cast on to a **40, 46, or 48 needle circular knitting machine** using scrap yarn. **Knit 5 rows in the scrap yarn.** Switch to the main color yarn leaving a very long yarn tail. **Knit 100 rows in the first color.** Switch to the second color. **Knit 100 rows in the second color.** Switch back to the scrap yarn. **Knit 5 rows in the scrap yarn.** Continue knitting until the work falls off the needles.

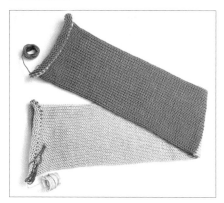

Then, follow the instructions in **Step 2** on **Page 22** to graft the ends of the knit tube together, and remove the scrap yarn.

After you've grafted the ends together, secure the yarn tails with a few good knots and hide the tails in the center of the knitting. Tour two-tone cowl is complete! Twist the cowl in half when worn, as shown here:

SINGLE-COLOR COWL:

Cast on to a **40, 46, or 48 needle circular knitting machine** using scrap yarn. **Knit 5 rows in the scrap yarn.** Switch to the main color yarn, leaving a very long yarn tail. **Knit 200 rows in the main color yarn.** Switch back to the scrap yarn. **Knit 5 rows in the scrap yarn.** Continue knitting until the work falls off the needles.

Then, follow the instructions in **Step 2** on **Page 22** to graft the ends of the knit tube together, and remove the scrap yarn.

STRIPED COWL:

Cast on to a **40, 46, or 48 needle circular knitting machine** using scrap yarn. **Knit 5 rows in the scrap yarn.** Switch to the main color yarn leaving a very long yarn tail. *Knit 10 rows in the first color. Knit 10 rows in the second color*. Repeat from * to * until you reach **200 rows**. Switch back to the scrap yarn. **Knit 5 rows in the scrap yarn.** Continue knitting until the work falls off the needles.

Then, follow the instructions in **Step 2** on **Page 22** to graft the ends of the knit tube together, and remove the scrap yarn.

SCARF:

Cast on to a **40, 46, or 48 needle circular knitting machine** using scrap yarn. **Knit 5 rows in the scrap yarn.** Switch to the main color yarn leaving a long yarn tail. **Knit 300 rows in the main color yarn.** Switch back to the scrap yarn. **Knit 5 rows in the scrap yarn.** Then, cut the scrap yarn and continue knitting until the work falls off the needles.

Then, use a crochet hook to seam the ends closed and remove the scrap yarn. (See Page 4 for details). If preferred, add fringe to the ends of the scarf.

The scarf shown here measures approximately 60". If you'd like a longer scarf, knit more rows. If you'd like a shorter scarf, knit fewer rows. Keep in mind that the scarf may stretch over time.

LONG STRIPED SCARF:

Cast on to a **40, 46, or 48 needle circular knitting machine** using scrap yarn. **Knit 5 rows in the scrap yarn.** Switch to the main color yarn leaving a long yarn tail. **Knit 20 rows in each color** until you reach **300-400 rows.** (For reference, the scarf shown below was knit with 400 rows). Switch back to the scrap yarn. **Knit 5 rows** in the scrap yarn. Then, cut the scrap yarn and continue knitting until the work falls off the needles.

Use a crochet hook to seam the ends closed and remove the scrap yarn. (See Page 4 for details). If preferred, add fringe to the ends of the scarf.

NOTES:

Scarves and cowls made with circular knitting machines are very easy to customize to your preferred length. The cowls included here fit snuggly when doubled up. If you'd like the cowl to have more room when doubled up, simply knit more rows. (For example, you could try a 300 row cowl).

The width of the scarves and cowls will be determined by the number of needles on the knitting machine. For example, a scarf made on a 40 needle circular knitting machine will be narrower than a scarf made on a 46 or 48 needle circular knitting machine. Keep in mind that some of these cowls and scarves required 2 skeins of yarn (250 yards/5oz each) to complete.

Matching Sets

Here are some examples of matching sets that were creating using the patterns in this book. You can mix and match the patterns in this book using similar color combinations to create matching sets.

Black & Pink Matching Set
Hat: "Adjustable Width Knitting Machine Hat", Size Small
Mittens: "Family Sized Mittens", Adult Size Small/Medium
Cowl: 200 rows on a 46 needle circular knitting machine
Yarn: *Heartland*™ Yarn from Lion Brand® Yarn

Black & Gold Matching Set
Hat: "Adjustable Width Knitting Machine Hat", Size Small
Mittens: "Family Sized Mittens", Adult Size Small/Medium
Cowl: 100 rows in black, 100 rows in gold on a 46 needle knitting machine
Yarn: *Heartland*™ Yarn from Lion Brand® Yarn

Halloween Matching Set
Hat: "Adjustable Width Knitting Machine Hat", Size Small
Mittens: "Family Sized Mittens", Adult Size Small/Medium
Cowl: 100 rows in black, 100 rows in orange on a 46 needle circular knitting machine
Yarn: *Heartland*™ Yarn from Lion Brand® Yarn

Valentine's Day Matching Set
Hat: "Adjustable Width Knitting Machine Hat", Size Small
Mittens: "Family Sized Mittens", Adult Size Small/Medium
Cowl: *10 rows red, 10 rows pink* and repeated from * to * until 200 rows on a 46 needle circular knitting machine
Yarn: *Heartland*™ Yarn from Lion Brand® Yarn

Example Photos

If you are brainstorming color combinations, here are some examples of hats and mittens that were created using the patterns in this book. The hearts were added to the mittens in the center using the Duplicate Stitch.

Share your work!
@dianalevineknits
dianalevineknits.com

Made in United States
Troutdale, OR
11/12/2024

24703543R00031